My Love for You Is Everywhere

A Book on Co-Parenting Little Hearts

Written by Melissa Diaz

Illustrated by María Tuti

Halo
PUBLISHING
INTERNATIONAL

Halo Publishing International
7550 W IH-10 #800, PMB 2069,
San Antonio, TX 78229

First Edition, May 2025
ISBN: 978-1-63765-730-0
Library of Congress Control Number: 2024925560

Halo Publishing International is a self-publishing company that publishes adult fiction and non-fiction, children's literature, self-help, spiritual, and faith-based books. Do you have a book idea you would like us to consider publishing? Please visit www.halopublishing.com for more information.

For all those who have experienced
an upbringing through separation
and for those who are barely
beginning their journeys.

May this book bring your heart ease.

It doesn't matter that you have two homes
or that we have to share your weekends.

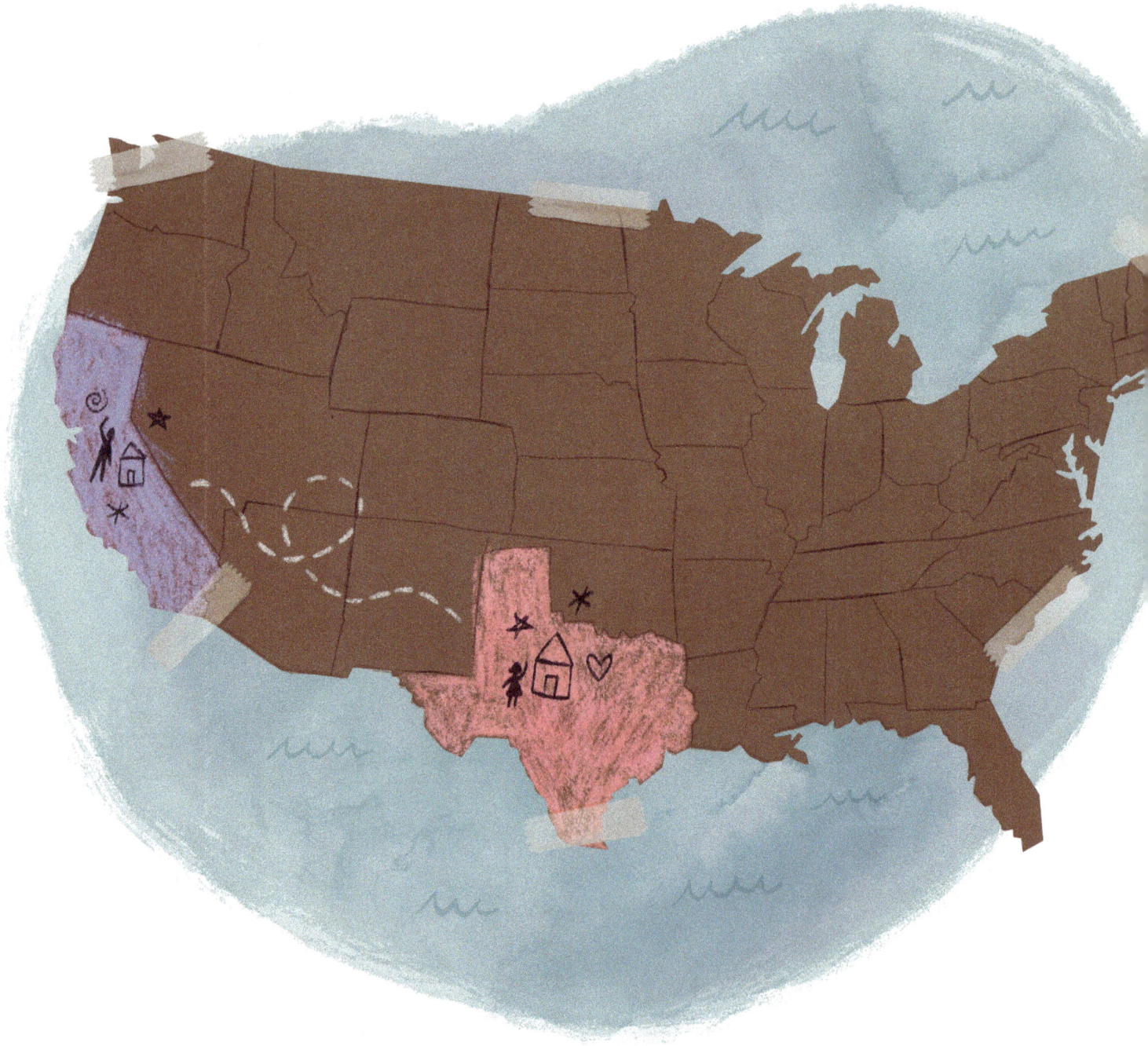

It doesn't matter if you're here or there.

Just remember that we care.

It doesn't matter if you pack a bag
or show up empty-handed...

I get to see you, my precious baby.

My heart is whole, and my arms are full,
whenever you are near.

It doesn't matter what your friends may say
or if they don't understand.

Just remember that **YOU** are our
pride and joy, no matter here or there.

On those days that you wake up sad
and missing this home,
remember that your family loves you.

I hope, when you're out
having adventures without me,
that your heart is happy and
that your giggle is loud.

In those moments,
I want you to remember
that you make me so very proud.

Just know, wherever you are,
either here or there...

My love for you is everywhere.

www.ingramcontent.com/pod-product-compliance
Lightning Source LLC
Chambersburg PA
CBHW060800150426
42813CB00058B/2771